BADMINTON

in a week

Barbara

Headway · Hodder & Stoughton

ACKNOWLEDGEMENTS

The author would like to thank Harry Jarvis for all his guidance. The author and publishers would like to thank Roddy Paine and Louis Ross for the photographs, and all the players who modelled for them.

For Emma

British Library Cataloguing in Publication Data
Jones, Barbara
  Badminton in a week. – (Sports in a week)
  I. Title   II. Series
  000.0

ISBN 0 340 55953 5

First published 1992

© 1992 Barbara M Jones

Typeset by Rowland Phototypesetting Ltd, Bury St Edmunds, Suffolk. Printed in Hong Kong for the educational publishing division of Hodder and Stoughton Ltd, Mill Road, Dunton Green, Sevenoaks, Kent by Colorcraft Ltd.

CONTENTS

INTRODUCTION

BADMINTON FOR ALL

Badminton is played throughout the world, at all levels from beginner to international, for a variety of reasons.

It is relatively easy to get started; it's exciting and you can make rapid progress in a short time, particularly if you get suitable help.

Badminton is a superb game for boys, girls, men and women from junior to senior citizen, for able bodied and for people with disabilities.

Many areas have special provision for ethnic minority groups. It is common for women only groups to have classes in sports centres, particularly in the daytime. Crêche facilities are often available.

Many players turn to badminton when they give up other sports and, once they realise what this outstanding game can offer them usually wish they could turn back the clock.

Two players of similar standard can have a thoroughly enjoyable game and can learn together, although it is advisable to join a class and have a qualified coach to help you establish good habits right from the start.

There will be no need to worry about the weather. You can organise your own play by making a private booking at a leisure centre or you can join a club where you can have fun and enjoyment in a social or competitive situation which can lead to an improved feeling of well being, thereby enhancing your quality of life.

You need minimum equipment to get started and only one other person to play singles or you can play as a four in level doubles (same sex) or mixed doubles.

When you take up badminton, you may have some natural talent that makes certain aspects of the game relatively easy for you to pick up. Skills from other sports can sometimes contribute to your speed of learning techniques which are specific to badminton.

As well as suggesting a logical sequence for the beginner to follow, the advice given can also be used by players who aspire to greater heights, to increase their knowledge and polish their skills with a view to improving personal performance. The guidelines can also be used by teachers and coaches.

In a week

The time spent practising during this week will open the doors to a wealth of opportunities for self expression through delicate touch and explosive power, fleetness of foot and alertness of mind. Your improved level of play will no doubt motivate you to want to continue to practise on a regular basis as new challenges occur.

Although practice makes perfect is a well-known saying, you should bear in mind that only quality practice makes perfect and it may take many years to become a perfect player.

How to start

You may decide to go along with a friend to your local sports centre to learn the game, following the step by step instructions. However this can be a long, slow process. By far the best way to make rapid progress in a week is to enrol for a residential course where, along with others of a similar standard, you can learn more quickly under the skilful guidance of experienced coaches. Your mistakes won't worry you when you see others in a similar position and you can learn with and from each other in a social setting.

Coaching can direct and accelerate progress

Where to play

If you decide to learn independently, call in at, or telephone your local leisure centre to find out the procedure for booking a court. Each centre will have its own system of booking and paying for courts. Booking is often permitted one week in advance. Reduced court fees may be available for off peak periods.

INTRODUCTION

Badminton Information Sources

WHO	WHAT	HOW
Local Education Authority	Adult education classes	Telephone Directory; Library; Education Office
Local Leisure Services	Sports centre courses; day, evening, weekend	Telephone Directory; Library; Leisure Services Office; Sports centres
Sports Council Regional Offices	Information on courses; Contact names and addresses	Telephone Directory
Badminton Association of England (BA of E)	Personal performance courses at various levels; Courses for coaches; Courses for umpires; Information regarding: Events; Regional co-ordinators; County associations; Books; Laws of the game; Videos	Bradwell Road, Loughton Lodge, Milton Keynes, MK8 9LA Telephone: 0908 568822

Preparation

Before your week of badminton starts, you can do some preparation which will make things easier for you when you begin. It's best to have your own racket, so make sure you know what to look for. The same applies to badminton shoes and clothing, although you don't have to buy everything at once. You will be able to get by with some casual sportswear. If you know someone who plays or coaches ask them for advice. Many shops sell leisure clothing and equipment but some specialist shops are also able to give advice and offer services such as repairs and re-stringing of rackets.

Choosing a racket

Choosing and caring for your own racket should be an act of love. Take your time and make sure that the racket not only looks good but feels right for you. After all, your racket will be the weapon with which you express yourself.

INTRODUCTION

Test the balance of the racket by placing it on your forefinger mid way along the shaft

The appearance of the racket plus the brand name will undoubtedly be the first things to catch your eye but rather like a new romance you have to find out if you are suited to each other.

Modern rackets are made from steel, aluminium, carbon fibre, ceramic, boron, kevlar or a combination of these. Consequently they are very light in weight. The shaft should be slightly flexible to give added power to your strokes although too flexible a shaft can lead to loss of control in hitting. A good racket will be well balanced and will not feel too heavy in either the head or the handle.

The strings in your racket can be gut or synthetic. The latter are usually harder wearing and technology has helped to produce synthetics which give a similar feel to gut. Test the tension of the strings by pressing your thumbs against them. They should feel firm to your touch.

Grip size is really important as is the quality of the grip itself because it's from the grip that you control the racket face. So many people use a grip size that is too big for their hand which forces them to hold the racket in the palm instead of in the fingers. To test for grip size place your thumb and forefinger round the handle until they touch. There should still be a small gap between the handle and the fleshy part of your hand between your thumb and forefinger.

Whether you use a leather or a towelling grip is a matter of personal preference but remember to check it regularly and replace it from time to time.

Having taken time and possibly having spent between £30–£60 on a quality racket, do look after it. Keep it in a racket head cover when not in use and never leave it near a radiator or exposed to excessive cold or bright sunlight.

Shuttles

Shuttles will be provided on a course but if you are organising your own practices, you will need to buy some. Many clubs and leagues use plastic shuttles, although top competition is with feather shuttles. They can be purchased from sports shops, sports centre shops or vending machines. A coloured band indicates the speed of synthetic shuttles; blue for medium speed which is the most used and red for a faster speed which is used in colder playing conditions.

Clothing

Look good, feel good is a true saying and can be applied to many occasions. If you take a pride in your appearance each time you step onto the badminton court, not only will you look competent but your confidence will be higher. Comfort should be the first priority when choosing kit. You don't want to find yourself restricted in your movements by clothes that are too tight, nor do you want to be hampered by baggy clothing. Kit can be predominantly white or coloured and matching shirt, shorts or skirt and reinforced socks can be purchased in most department stores. A tracksuit is an essential part of every badminton player's wardrobe and a sweater can be a useful addition. Don't worry about buying everything at once. Most people will already possess some leisure clothing which will be suitable for starting off.

Shoes

Your feet will do an awful lot of work during your badminton life, so make sure that you look after them. Invest in a pair of good badminton shoes and reap the rewards rather than the problems which can arise from playing in some training or road running shoes. Footwear should be light in weight, give adequate support and protection and should provide flexibility and grip.

Traditional white or coloured clothing can look equally smart

Final preparations

Prepare a small first aid kit containing scissors and plasters; a drinks bottle for a soft drink; a towel and a small bag in which to carry these, a

INTRODUCTION

spare racket if possible, a spare grip and a change of kit and you're ready to begin.

The badminton court

A basic knowledge of the court layout and an understanding of which lines are used at various stages in the game will be useful to you when you play, so study the diagram before you go to practise.

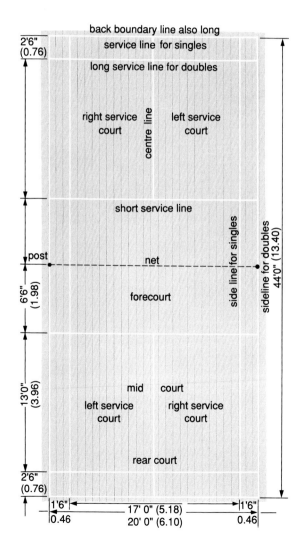

MONDAY

GETTING STARTED

> **Today's Aims**
> Familiarise yourself with the warm up;
> Find out how to control the racket face and head;
> Play a game.

Preparing to play

Allow yourself time for suitable preparations by arriving at the hall a little while before you are due to start. You may decide to change in the centre or you may prefer to wear your tracksuit over your badminton clothing to go to the hall. Wear alternative shoes and change into your badminton shoes inside the hall. Your playing shoes won't do their job properly if they have dirt, grit or damp on the soles and the court surface may also be affected to the detriment of all users.

Warm up

It's best to begin each session with a warm up which will get you mentally and physically ready for your activity. The duration and degree of warm up will be determined by your level of practice and play and by your own general fitness. Don't set off like a bull in a china shop. It's just as easy to overdo the warm up as it is to underdo it.

For a beginner, about five minutes of relaxed jogging followed by a similar length of time spent *slow* stretching should prevent or reduce the risk of injury from starting with cold muscles.

*Hold all stretches
for six seconds
Repeat each stretch
two to four times
Stretch to pain, not
through pain*

Getting to grips with your racket

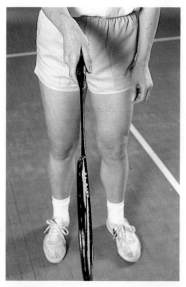

Your racket is the tool of your trade. The way you hold it will be crucial to the outcome of your shots, so make sure you develop the right habit from the start. Your grip controls the racket face which in turn determines the line of flight of the shuttle. Today look closely at the two main grips, forehand and backhand, and try them out.

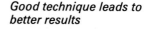

Good technique leads to better results

Checkpoints for forehand grip

Feel that you are holding the racket predominantly with your fingers, rather than the palm of your hand. Your fingers should be slightly spread out on the handle as you shake hands with your racket. The bottom of the V between your thumb and forefinger should be on the top bevel in line with the rim of the racket.

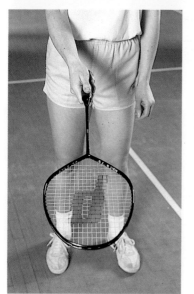

To change to the backhand grip, rotate your racket between your thumb and forefinger until the pad of your thumb is on the broad bevel of your racket pointing towards the T, or throat of the racket

MONDAY

Changing grip

Be prepared to experiment with changing from forehand to backhand
grip. At first you will need to look to check, but eventually you should be
able to feel the correct position of your fingers and thumb on your
racket. The tiny variations of your fingers for subtle control can take a
player into a new dimension of play, so try to be aware of this from the
start.

Solo practice

For your first practice, find a space so that there is no danger of clashing
with anyone else. Using the forehand grip and the forehand face of your
racket, try hitting the shuttle upwards into the air. Keep your eye on the
shuttle both whilst it is in the air and as you hit it.

As the shuttle falls back towards the strings of your racket, drop your
hand back at the wrist. In badminton terms this is referred to as *cocking
the hand*. To hit the shuttle, uncock your hand and feel that you are using
a *tap* action to send the shuttle into space.

Concentrate on watching carefully and try to hit with the centre of the
racket each time. Some rackets have an emblem on the strings, so you
can pick your target zone for a central point.

*Keep your eye on the shuttle as
it falls and as you hit it*

*In the ready position your
hand must be cocked*

Judgement

Control your racket head by varying the degree of wrist action that you
use. This enables you to hit the shuttle with a delicate touch obtained by
using a soft wrist action keeping the shuttle close to the racket, or gives

13

you the opportunity for a sharper, faster action sending the shuttle to greater heights.

Test your control by playing a sequence of low, medium and high hits. The sheer joy of hitting and controlling the shuttle begins with these simple practices and the principles can be carried forward as you develop further aspects of your game.

Change to the backhand grip and try out the same practice using the backhand face of your racket.

Develop this practice so that you learn to change automatically from one grip to another as the occasion demands.

Wall practice

You can never beat the wall but you can become a better player by playing against it.

Standing one to two metres away from the wall, hit the shuttle against the wall, beginning with 10 forehand hits, then 10 backhand hits, using the correct grip each time.

As you get control, make the changes of grip more frequent. Use underarm, overarm and sidearm hits, so that you develop a range of useful hitting actions within the grip change practice. This can become a

Regular practice against the wall is effective practice at all levels of play

MONDAY

daily practice. Five minutes a day will soon sharpen your reflexes.

Your focus of attention in any practice needs to be clear. At first your attention will be directed to a particular aspect of play but as you progress you will have your own thoughts and will be able to apply your own focus within a practice.

Co-operation practices

The next step will be to practise with a partner, so go onto the court on the opposite side of the net to your partner.

Stand about halfway between the net and the backline in one half of the court. Hit the shuttle between you at a fairly steady pace.

Explore the different ways in which you can hit the shuttle. It's important to hit the shuttle to each other, because you are trying to help each other. Later on you'll be able to use your skills to compete against each other.

Try to develop a pattern of:
Ready Hold your racket in front of your body, hand cocked.
Prepare and hit Take the racket into the striking position and with a continuous action, strike the shuttle.
Recover Return to the ready position.

Concentration

At first concentrate on watching the shuttle. Try to pick up the line of flight of the shuttle as soon as it leaves your partner's racket and move to where you think you need to be, then immediately switch your attention to watching the shuttle as you hit it. See how many consecutive hits you and your partner can make between you without a mistake.

You should find yourself using the underarm, overarm and sidearm hitting actions that you practised against the wall, as you hit the shuttle upwards, downwards and flat.

Each rally should begin with an underarm hit from the first striker. After that, try to hit with your racket head above your hand whenever you can, since this can often give you an advantage in the game.

Practice – what's it all about?

Practices may sometimes look alike but the purpose of the practice may vary. It's a good idea to remind yourself about what you are trying to achieve within a practice. The next practice will be set up in the same way as the previous one but it will be about checking and changing your grip.

MONDAY

Rally with your partner from midcourt to midcourt. Use your forehand grip and face, whilst your partner uses the backhand. After 10 hits each, reverse the practice. Gradually decrease the number of hits with each grip until you can hit at random, from either side of and in front of your body, using the appropriate grip.

Beginning a stroke with the correct grip doesn't necessarily mean that you can maintain the grip throughout the stroke. Sweaty hands can lead to loss of grip, as can a worn or greasy racket grip, so take care of both of these possibilities by using talcum powder or a specialised substance for sweaty hands and by checking the quality of your racket grip and changing it when necessary.

Moving and hitting

All of the practices so far have been fairly static to give you the chance to improve your skills without being under pressure. No doubt you'll have itchy feet and will want to get the feel of real badminton which is often referred to as physical chess. In the next practice you'll get the chance to do this.

One of you acts as a feeder in this practice whilst the other is the player. The feeder begins each rally with the shuttle and hits the first shot towards the back or rearcourt. The purpose of the practice is to vary the way in which you use your racket head to hit the shuttle, making your partner move towards the forecourt and then back to the rearcourt.

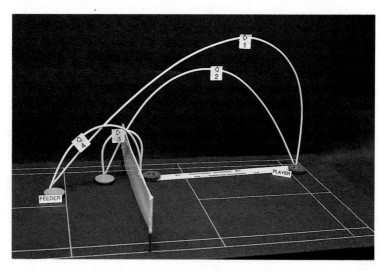

Feeder and player working together

MONDAY

Racket head control

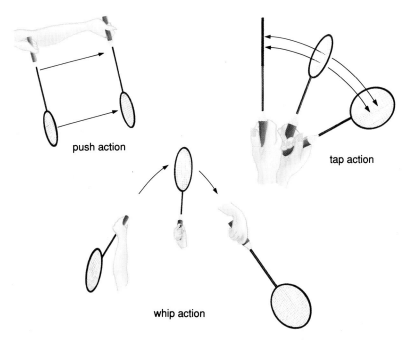

push action

tap action

whip action

Push, tap, whip actions

For shots played around the net area, from just below net height, restrict your wrist action to control your racket head. Keep your hand cocked back or allow it to partially uncock, giving the feeling of a *push* action.

To send your partner quickly to the rearcourt, uncock your hand but return it immediately into the cocked position, experiencing a *tap* action.

To give more height to the shuttle as you hit it towards the back of the court, use more of your arm and uncock your hand sharply at the end of the stroke, allowing your racket head to follow the line of flight of the shuttle, creating the feeling of a whip action.

After about three minutes, change roles with your partner.

Go through this practice about three times each, trying to improve your control and consistency with each turn. Knowing roughly where you will have to move to after each hit should mean that life is not too difficult for you at this stage of your development. Moving smoothly and trying to be in balance for each hit will help you, but you can look more closely at that later in the week.

MONDAY

For the final practice before you play a game, work as before, except, as the feeder, your choice of shots can be random rather than sequential. You can now put your newly learned skills to the test and see the effect that your shots have as you try to catch your partner out. Move your partner around the half court using a mixture of soft and strong hits. Your partner has now become your opponent and battle is about to commence.

After you have both had the chance to sample these practices, you can play a game.

Half court singles

Half court singles is an excellent game to start with. It gives you the opportunity to rally for longer than on a full court, to explore the length of the court and to engage in a tactical encounter.

Check the area of play, the rules of the game and then have a go.

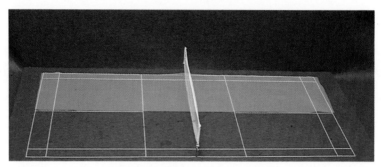

Area used for half court singles

The area between the front, or short, service line and the net will be *out* for service but *in* for the rest of the game. The side tramline which is not used at all in full court singles will be *out* for serve but *in* at all other times in this game.

Just in case you're in doubt, when serving or receiving serve, the short service line and the long service line (back boundary line in singles) count as *in* should any part of the shuttle land on any part of the line. The same rule applies to the other lines during the course of a game.

There is no line between the net and the centre point of the short service line, so if the shuttle lands in this area and you cannot say whether it was in or out, play a *let*.

To decide who has the choice of serving, not serving or choice of ends, spin the racket and respond to the call of rough or smooth by feeling along the bottom strings on the racket which are usually looped.

Alternatively, throw the shuttle up in the air. If it lands with the base pointing towards you, you have first choice. Your opponent can choose from whatever is left.

Serving and receiving serve

You must stand behind the short service line both when you are serving and when you are receiving serve. Stand about one metre back from the front service line. Server and receiver must not have a foot on any line and as the server you must keep a part of both feet in contact with the floor throughout the service action and you are not allowed to drag your foot along the floor.

Remember that you have to serve underarm. The precise regulations regarding service are detailed later (see chapter 2).

How to score

Scoring is similar to squash and volleyball, so if you are familiar with either of these games you will know that only the serving side can win a point. You continue to serve as long as your side is winning. If you lose the rally, the service passes over to the other side (service over) without loss of a point.

Girls and women play singles up to 11 points whilst boys and men play up to 15 points. In all cases, a formal match is usually the best of three games with setting.

Setting

In a game of 11 points, if the score is 9–9, the player who first reached that score has the choice to play *straight through* or to *set*. If you choose to set, the game restarts at 0–0 and the first player to win three points is the winner. Setting at 10–10, the first player to win two points is the winner. If setting is declined at 9–9, the option is still available to the relevant side at 10–10.

Checklist for setting

Total points in game	Setting available at	Points needed to win after setting
11	9–9	3
11	10–10	2
15	13–13	5
15	14–14	3

When you are with a group of players it's a good idea to play shortened games, like five points up or play for five minutes and then swap around.

In this way, you learn with and from each other and on a new course you meet new people.

Taking a break

With all this activity, you will find that you will need a drink from time to time. Have a break to take a sip of water or a soft, preferably non-fizzy, drink. Nature usually gives us adequate signals in life but in this case the signal of feeling thirsty comes a little too late. Take liquid on board early is a good philosophy.

Competing

You will already have become aware, even after this short space of time, of some of the tactics or strategies you can use when you are competing. To help you think about how to win the game, consider the following.

Within the rules of the game, you have to try to create a situation which enables you to hit the shuttle onto the floor in your opponent's court or forces them to hit the shuttle into the net or out of court. Your skill, intelligence and patience will be put to the test, but you are always a winner if you come off the court having played to the best of your ability and learned something.

Warming down

After a fairly strenuous session you will probably want to slip away to shower, change and relax. However, a few minutes at the end of each session looking after your body will be well invested time when you come to your next session.

Working will have raised your body temperature and it's best to let it drop gradually rather than suddenly, so put your tracksuit back on, or an extra layer of clothing of some kind.

The warm down is the reverse of the warm up although it consists of similar activities.

A gentle jog or walk followed by slow stretching of your muscles, similar to those at the start of the session, will be fine. With repeated hard work, muscles can shorten and stretching helps them to resume their normal length. Serious players work regularly to increase their range of flexibility, to give themselves scope to be more athletic in a game without putting themselves at risk.

TUESDAY

PLAYING SINGLES

Today's Aims

Revise and improve your warm up and your GCE (grip, cocked hand, eye on shuttle);
Develop your skill and understanding of:
The high serve;
Strokes played from the rearcourt;
Getting behind the shuttle;
Full court singles.

Today's warm up will follow the same basic procedure as before, except intersperse some backward running and some *chasse* movements with the jogging.

Backward running is fairly self explanatory but make sure that there are no obstacles behind you and take it steady so that you keep your balance.

Chasse style movement may be new to you; it's a form of side to side skips in which one foot repeatedly catches up with the other. You should practise with your right side leading and with your left side leading. Change from right to left every two steps.

GCE

Practise first against the wall and then on the court with your partner to revise and improve your grip, cocking of hand and your ability to keep your eye on the shuttle.

Using the half court principle, working from the midcourt position, you and your partner should hit the shuttle between you.

It's important to make contact with the shuttle in front of your body and to work whenever possible with your racket head above or to the side of your hand throughout the practice.

Angle of racket face

Your racket face should be square to the shuttle on impact, otherwise you will find yourself slicing or mis-hitting the shuttle.

Rotate your forearm as you hit, so that the palm of your hand is behind the racket on the forehand. On the backhand, the pad of your thumb behind your racket is the guiding point.

Tap and push practice

For the first few minutes try to develop the feeling of the tap action, rebounding your racket head after hitting the shuttle to resume the cocked hand position as quickly as possible. Try to hit the shuttle so that it skims the net. How close can you go?

Next, limit the uncocking of your hand to little or none, to improve your skill in the push action. The shuttle should again pass close to the net and travel towards your partner but it should begin to dip as it crosses the net. One measure of your success will be that your partner may have to drop their racket head below their hand to deal with your effective shot.

Keep your racket head above your hand whenever possible

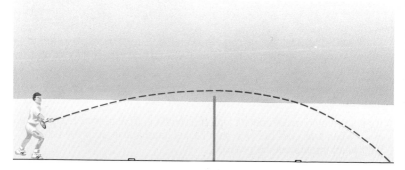

It's an advantage to get the shuttle low on the other side of the net

Battle of skills and wits

You're probably ready for a competitive practice now, so here's the chance for you to pit your wits and skill against each other.

Working in the area from just in front of the doubles long service line to the net, mix *pushes* and *taps*.

TUESDAY

You can score either as you do in badminton or with a point to the player who wins the rally, regardless of who served.

The scoring is secondary to the skill development. Nevertheless, you will want to enjoy the thrill of the game and if you want to increase your chances of winning you need to be up on your toes from the word go.

Ready, steady, go

Fleetness of foot and speed off the mark come from being ready and alert before and during a rally. It's no good having tree trunk legs with your feet firmly rooted to the spot.

Legs bent at the knees, weight on the balls of your feet and good posture are the outward signs. Inwardly, you need the alertness of a cat, watching and waiting for the moment to pounce on its victim.

Bent legs, ready to drive your feet into instant action

The high serve

The serve is the only stroke in the game which is entirely dependent on you, since nothing your opponent can do can physically affect it.

Aims of the high serve

- To move your opponent as far back as possible in the rearcourt, giving the least chance to attack you with her reply.
- To create a space in the forecourt.
- To give your opponent the problem of having to hit a shuttle falling vertically from a great height.

Before you begin to practise this stroke, make sure you know and understand the laws relating to service, so that you don't develop a foul serve.

Laws of service

- Stand completely inside your own service area, without any part of your feet touching a line.
- Keep some part of both feet stationary and in contact with the floor.
- Do not deliberately delay serving so as to gain an unfair advantage.
- Use only one continuous forward hitting action.
- The first contact must be on the base of the shuttle.
- The whole of your racket head must be below the lowest point of your racket hand on impact with the shuttle.
- No part of the shuttle should be struck from above your waist.

Service faults result in loss of serve, so make sure that your serve is legal and earn yourself a good reputation

Serving high

Develop a serving routine

Take up your position. Stand about one metre behind the short service line. There's no golden rule regarding the precise distance; once you've practised a few serves you can adjust your position to suit your needs.

The basic action used for the high serve is a fairly simple one in that it's similar to throwing a ball forwards and upwards, with one hand, using an underarm action

Keypoints Check these *one at a time*.

- Decide whereabouts you want the shuttle to land.
- Try to feel relaxed, particularly in your grip. It's fatal to strangle your racket at any time.
- Stand slightly sideways on, in a comfortable position, feet approximately shoulder width apart, with your weight predominantly on your back foot.
- Hold the shuttle by the skirt or feathers, slightly out in front of you.
- Take your arm and racket back into position for a big underarm throw, remembering how important it is to have your hand cocked at the wrist.
- Try to release the shuttle from the same place each time you serve.
- Throw your racket head through the shuttle, feeling that you are using an underarm whip action and let your racket head follow the line of flight of the shuttle.
- Turn your body to face forwards as your weight transfers from your back to your front foot.
- Keep your eye on the shuttle throughout the action, possibly for a split second longer than you think you need to.

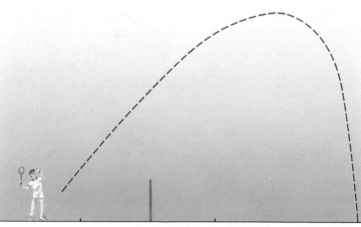

Consistency of length and height are crucial and to achieve these you need frequent practice

TUESDAY

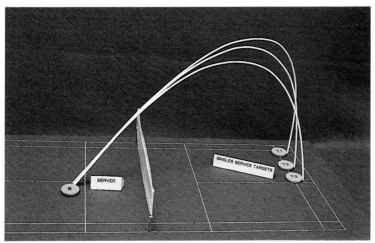

You may want to test your accuracy, so put a target in the back tramlines to test yourself for the singles high service. Don't fall into the trap of neglecting the height, otherwise your practice is not really one of high serving

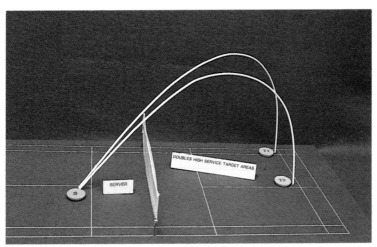

A similar situation can be practised relating to the doubles game but the target will be placed just in front of the inside back tramline, which is the long service line in doubles

The use of the high serve in doubles may be limited unless your opponents have a weak attack, or you have a strong, effective defence.

TUESDAY

Laws

Serve from the right-hand court whenever your score is love or an even number and from the left-hand court whenever your score is an odd number.

Serve into the diagonally opposite court and stand in the diagonally opposite court when your opponent is serving.

Court positioning – singles

After serving, you need to get into the habit of taking up a position on the court from which you can move to cover any reply that your opponent can hit. Today, relate this position to full court singles.

Having served high and deep into the court, straddle the centre line in the midcourt or move fractionally to one side if you have served out wide to the corner, so that your position slightly favours the straight reply, since a cross court reply will take a split second longer

Put your service to the test

To give yourself the opportunity to use your newly acquired skills, play full court singles using only the high serve each time you start a rally.

Remember that the side tramlines are not part of the singles court.

TUESDAY

Prepare to reply to the high serve

If your opponent is going to force you to the rearcourt with an effective high serve, you must equip yourself to be equally effective with your reply, so check the forehand overhead shots.

The golden rule in this situation really must be to get behind the shuttle in a balanced position

Rearcourt strokes

Be poised, yet relaxed, as you prepare to hit either a clear, a smash or a dropshot.

Be decisive about your choice of stroke, since badminton is no game for hesitators.

Don't give any telltale signals that will give your opponent an inkling of what shot you are about to play.

Present the same picture for all these strokes; once you've learned how to play them you will be able to threaten your opposition by preparing for a smash but will sometimes play a deceptive clear or dropshot.

Keypoints

- At the back of the court step back so that your weight is mainly on your racket leg (right-handed player, right leg and vice versa).
- Use your non-racket arm for relaxed counter balance and as a pointer at the shuttle.
- Turn your shoulders as you pull your racket back, rather like an archer pulling back an arrow in a bow.
- From this strong, sideways-on position, drop your racket head back, with your elbow bent and your hand cocked and with one fast, smooth action, starting from your feet and finishing with your fingers, throw your racket head upwards and forwards at the shuttle.

- As you are throwing, turn your body to face the net and rotate your forearm to meet the shuttle with your racket head square on. Control your racket head to create the desired stroke, uncocking your hand and following through the shuttle for the clear or the smash; for drop shots, use either the tap action or the push action.
- Bring your racket leg through to complete each stroke which will simultaneously take you on your way back to a position on court from which you can cover possible replies.

Prepare, hit and follow through, then immediately return to base

To practise your technique in the overhead strokes, it's necessary to have a partner who can hit the shuttle high towards the rearcourt. If you haven't got someone who can do this well enough, they may be able to throw the shuttle so that your can practise or you can self feed by hitting the shuttle up high above you.

Alternate with your partner, practising first the overhead clears, then the smash and last but not least the dropshots.

Hand feed for your partner, standing in a safe position

Focus of attention

Concentrate on a keypoint of the action and give yourself the opportunity to improve that aspect before moving on to another. Sometimes you may need to isolate one part of the stroke, to try to improve it and then go back to the whole stroke practice. It's better to be patient and aim to get it right, rather than rush through a practice and achieve nothing. Regular, quality practice is the key to improvement. When you're practising to improve your technique, think about how you are performing the stroke, rather than the outcome of it.

How accurate are you?

The next stage will be to test your accuracy and consistency, so aim at some targets.

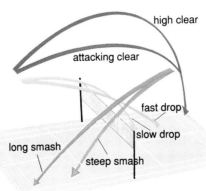

Trajectories and target areas for clears, smash and drop shots. Keep a daily record of your accuracy

Moving your partner

To combine stroke and movement, set up the following practice with your partner. At first limit yourselves to the half court, as you did when you played half court singles. Take up your position in the rearcourt; you are called the *feeder*.

Your partner takes up position in the midcourt on the opposite side of the net and begins each rally with a high serve. To begin with, use a clear alternating with a drop shot, to move your partner alternately to the back and front of the court.

Decision making

To explore the effect of these shots in the game, develop the previous practice from a simple to a more complex one which will involve decision making. When you are the feeder, you may elect to play either the clear or the drop shot at any time.

The strokes as moves in the game

As the feeder you will soon begin to realise:

- The standard clear moves your opponent to the rearcourt, creating a space in the forecourt.
- The attacking clear, particularly when used in conjunction with effective drop shots, can put pressure on the opposition and may even be an outright winning shot.

When you change roles within this practice and you become the worker, you will find the high defensive clear a valuable stroke which can get you off the hook in a tight situation by creating time to recover.

Your drop shots should be varied in pace and placement. The slower drop will pull your opponent close to the net but you will give away the advantage if your opponent can take the shuttle close to the tape. Your aim should be to force your opponent to hit the shuttle from as low down as possible. The fast drop will travel more quickly to its destination but will not bring your opponent as far forward on the court.

Developing the practice

Later, you can incorporate the smash into the practice. It may not be too easy to smash through the opposition in the half court, unless your opponent has hit short of a length. However, you may be able to force a weak reply or even an error from your opponent as a result of your smash.

TUESDAY

Points to consider

- Placement – at the body, to the forehand, to the backhand.
- Placement and power – a combination of these is usually more effective than all-out power.

Deception

Deception of stroke plays a major part, so remember to make your approach to each stroke the same. Your dropshot is likely to be more effective if your opponent is backing off to cover your smash or your attacking clear.

Feeder/worker

Alternate each practice frequently, so that each of you gets the chance to be the feeder and then the worker.

Whilst you are working, you must try to hold your skills together under some pressure. As the feeder, you have the ideal opportunity to practise and polish your skills whilst gaining insight into their tactical use in the game. As your confidence and competence grow, you can progress from the half court practices and half court game, to the full court.

Body skills

The skills of moving on the court are just as important as the skills of hitting but can be a neglected area, particularly in the self-taught player. Some players will be natural scramblers but an efficient player will move smoothly, have a good sense of balance and will be able to combine some of the body skills of a gymnast, a dancer and an explosive athlete as they twist, turn, jump and land safely as they travel around the court.

In the next practice, try out ways of travelling, starting and stopping.

This singles player is poised, with bent legs, ready to receive service by going either forwards or backwards, in response to the serve. The aim will be to get quickly into a balanced striking position

Travelling

When you are receiving serve, your body starting stance will already be sideways on. If your opponent serves high and deep, you must, immediately the shuttle is struck, and not before, push away from the ground to move to the back of the court so that you are behind the shuttle and in balance when you hit it.

The chasse style movement which you did in the warm up lends itself quite naturally to this situation.

To help you stop in balance at the back of the court, reach back with your racket leg. You should now be in the hitting position for one of the forehand overhead strokes which you practised earlier. Play an imaginary stroke and return, moving smoothly and fluently to the centre of the court.

Do this several times. Ask your partner to observe and comment on your movement. Perhaps they can grade you on a scale of 1 to 5 on your quality of movement based on their opinion.

Aspects to look for

- Moving smoothly and softly
- Good posture
- Good balance

Within a rally when you need to move from your base to the rearcourt, you can either run backwards and turn to get sideways on, or your first movement can be a turn to a sideways position and then proceed as before.

It's useful to practise more than one way of travelling. You may have a preference for a particular style but an alternative style will double your options. The main criteria are the quality and the effectiveness of your movement.

Practise moving from a ready position to a hitting position; shadow the hitting action, then move back into a ready position.

Build up from one repetition to several continuous repetitions.

As with all aspects of your badminton, regular quality practice in which you understand why and how you are practising combined with the patience and determination to get it right eventually is a stepping stone to success.

After isolating and improving your movement, combine moving with hitting, your aim being to get back behind the shuttle in an early balanced position.

TUESDAY

Full court singles

Today consider how to set about achieving the aims of the game.

If you want to hit the shuttle onto the floor in your opponent's court, you will need to play a series of shots which will eventually force a short length reply from your opponent, giving you the opportunity to hit a successful downward shot. Each stroke is regarded as a move in the game.

Don't jump to the conclusion that the only downwards winning stroke is the smash. A kill from the net or a delicate drop shot can be equally effective, particularly if it's played with deception. The key lies in the opportunity and the stroke selection. This will vary from one opponent to another since each will have varying strengths and weaknesses.

Some players are by nature defensive in their approach to the game. They are usually prepared to rally until their opponent makes a mistake. However, try to force your opponent into making that mistake by using a range of shots that will put their strokes under pressure. If there is a weakness, and there usually is, try to exploit it.

If you feel that you are fitter than your opponent, you can rally to tire them until their skills of moving or effective hitting break down.

Conditioned games

These games take you into the final stage of practising before you truly test yourself against an opponent.

Play a game of singles without using your smash. In this game you will learn to use that all important length of the court.

An alternative to this is that you are only allowed to smash after you have made your opponent a) place at least one foot in the back tramlines or b) reach with their racket in front of the short service line. This condition applies to each rally.

To learn how to use angles on the court and to combine using the length and width, before being allowed to smash, you must make your opponent move completely into one half of the court.

Think about your own strengths and weaknesses and if possible about your opponent's. Armed with this information, you can plan how to play against them.

For the final part of today, play some games of singles. Play as well and as hard as you can, so that you feel satisfied with yourself when you finish, but above all enjoy your badminton.

Just one final reminder – don't forget to warm down. It's all part of the daily routine.

WEDNESDAY

LEVEL DOUBLES

Today's Aims

Improve your shuttle control.
Learn how to low serve.
Find out about and practise strokes from the forecourt.
Improve your body skills.
Learn the basic court positioning in level doubles.

Shuttle control

Since badminton is a game of accuracy, the more opportunities you have of learning to control the shuttle in a variety of ways, the more options you will have in a game. With insight into how and why you play certain shots, you can help yourself to be effective.

Mental control

Efficient players will think on their feet. Whatever happens, remain calm. Too much emotion may inhibit your skill.

Challenge yourself

The daily routine of warm up, racket and body skills practices, may make you think that each day is the same, but this is far from true. Each day is a challenge to be better than you were before. The number of ways in which you can practise these skills is numerous. Simply working with another person will make a difference, since everyone has a unique style. Style should be founded on good basics. There's no substitute for these in any sport.

Applying your skills

When you progress from your general racket skills to specific stroke skills practice, you will be well rewarded. Your daily practice to develop the feeling of the push, tap or whip actions can be applied to the strokes and the more you practise changing from one grip to another, the more automatic this will become when you play.

Below the belt

Since one of today's aims is to learn about the level doubles game, it will be essential to acquire a tape skimming low serve which will give your side an advantage at the start of the rally. If you can make your opponent strike the shuttle from below the tape, or better still below the belt, you will have the advantage.

Remember the serving laws

Please note that it is not a fault if the shuttle touches the net as it crosses during service, or at any other stage of the game.

You may have a preference for one type of serve but an alternative gives you a choice, so learn and practise both forehand and backhand serving

Forehand low serve

Keypoints

- Stand in a relaxed, balanced, slightly sideways on position.
- Some players stand as close as possible to the front line; others stand just a little further back. The closer you are, the less time your opponent has to *read* the shot.
- It's best to keep the hitting action fairly short and simple, so take your racket back just a short distance, making sure that your hand is cocked back.
- Decide where along the front line you are going to serve to.
- Hold the shuttle slightly out in front of you and, to develop a consistent action, release the shuttle from the same place each time.
- Use a push action to guide the shuttle as you sway your weight through from your back foot to your front foot.
- Keep your eye on the shuttle throughout the action.

Target practice

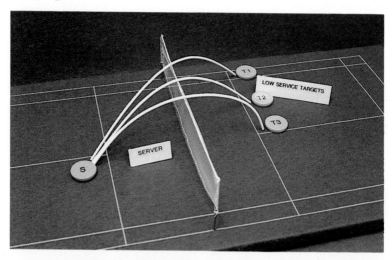

Once you've got the feel of the action, get your partner to place their racket somewhere along the front service line

Push the shuttle low over the net onto the target. No matter where the target is, it's best to prepare as if you are serving to the T, so that, in the game, you can leave your opponent guessing as to precisely where you will serve

The shortened grip

Using a shortened grip can give you greater control of your racket head in certain situations. Try it when you serve

WEDNESDAY

Backhand low serve

Groove the action

Most players stand racket foot up to the front service line, using either the standard or the shortened backhand grip. Hold the racket out in front of you and then take the shuttle out in front of the racket.

By following this pattern you will be able to pull the racket back before you begin your forward approach to the shuttle, thereby avoiding two forward movements which constitute a fault. As before, pick your spot and push your racket head through the shuttle towards it, keeping your hand cocked back in case you need to make a last, split second change of action to flick the shuttlecock past or over an over-enthusiastic receiver.

You can rehearse all day long but your serve must be put to the test of being effective against an opponent who will be trying to put pressure on you, usually by taking up a threatening position as close as possible to the front service line

Basic principles when serving

- Take your time.
- Relax.
- Mentally rehearse the serve.
- Feel confident.

As soon as your serving action is completed, you need to be up on your toes, with your racket up, eager to intercept any low reply.

One step at a time

There are many ways to practise and many things to think about but you can't think about them all at the same time. At first work on your technique and then develop ideas based on tactical insight.

39

WEDNESDAY

Where to serve to

The area that you serve to will partly depend on where your opponent stands. Somewhere there will be a weakness. It's up to you to find it.

An obvious weakness may be that your opponent stands too close in and can be beaten outright or caught off balance by your late, well-disguised flick.

Remember that the inside back tramline is the limiting service line in doubles and that the side tramlines are *in*.

Your opponent may stand too close to the centre line, particularly a right-handed player receiving in their right court trying to cover a weak backhand. Try serving low and wide into the side tramlines.

A less obvious weakness may be a point along the front service line from where your opponent makes a predictable reply which either you or your partner are ready to take advantage of.

Be prepared to vary your serve, not only from forehand to backhand but also by moving your base forwards, backwards or sideways to create different angles and trajectories.

Now you can try out your low serve against a receiver to see if you can serve well under pressure.

You can try this in a simple serve and return practice and later you can play a conditioned game in which you are restricted to low serving only.

All these experiences can be tucked away in your memory box and used in the game situation but remember to practise them regularly or they may become rusty.

Strokes from the forecourt

Net kill

Whether you are playing singles or doubles, the principle of attack should be uppermost in your thinking. The first stroke from the forecourt which follows this principle is the *net kill*.

> ### Keypoints
>
> * Play with your racket foot forwards, so that you can reach further.
> * Hold your racket above, but close to, the net with your hand cocked.
> * Use a tap action so that your racket is swiftly back in position just in case your opponent manages to return the shuttle.

WEDNESDAY

The aim of the net kill is to hit the shuttle from above net height onto the floor on the opposite side of the net. Unlike the name suggests, the net kill is a delicate shot played with efficient precision on either backhand or forehand

Laws

Your racket must be on your own side of the net when you contact the shuttle but is allowed to pass over the line of the net in following through, providing you do not touch the net with either your racket or your person. No part of you or your racket is allowed to pass under the line of the net.

Feeding

Multi-shuttle feeding will give you the opportunity to hit many shuttles in a short space of time and will also hopefully encourage you to keep your racket up between hits. A low racket will undoubtedly mean a missed opportunity to put the shuttle on the floor.

One player throws the shuttle upwards to just above the net for the other player. Feed shuttles in rapid succession. Work in sets of 10, until five sets have been completed and then change over.

Strokes and movement

Practise the technical aspects of any stroke followed by the appropriate movement before and after the stroke and then put them together and you have a game related practice. Assess the possible replies that your opponent can make and you're in business.

41

WEDNESDAY

To give yourself the best possible chance to see and reach the shuttle as soon as it crosses the net, you need to be alert and agile, ready to step or jump into position. Chasse back to your ready position between shots

Isolate the movement needed to play the net kill. As before, you and your partner can assist each other.

Check:

- Bend legs in preparation.
- Weight on balls of feet.
- Racket up; non-racket arm used for counter balance.
- Good posture.
- Take one or two steps finishing with your racket leg towards the net.
- If you jump, travel upwards and forwards.
- Land lightly and in balance.
- Chasse back off the net.

You cannot possibly check all these aspects at once. Take each one in turn. Tell your partner what you are checking. Getting it right several times and eventually every time is the ultimate aim.

Net shots

If you are not in a position to play the net kill, you may want to play a *tight net* shot which may create an opportunity for you to kill any reply to the net area or may result in the shuttle being lifted to the rearcourt where, in doubles, your partner will deal with it effectively.

WEDNESDAY

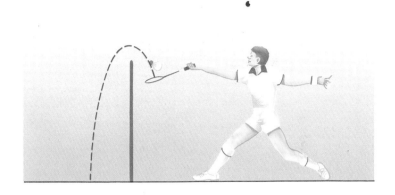

Think of net shots as upward shots. This means that your racket face should be placed under the shuttle. From this position push the shuttle gently upwards and slightly forwards so that it trickles over the net

Practise both forehand and backhand strokes

As in the net kill practice, get your partner to hand feed for you. This time your contact will be below net height, so the feed must be tighter to the net.

WEDNESDAY

Working as a team

When you play doubles you will share the responsibilities in the game with your partner. Sometimes you will be required to take care of and dominate the front of the court. In this situation the net kill and tight net shots will be an essential part of your game.

The front of court player has less time to see the shuttle than their partner and must consequently have faster reactions

To help improve your front of court play and to involve you in a practice which requires decision making, work in a group of three. As the first feeder throws the shuttle, move quickly towards the net, with your racket up ready to play a kill. If you are not quick enough to play this shot, play a tight net shot. When you get back to your base, the second feeder will throw the next shuttle.

Practise with care

Be prepared to take care. All too often players and feeders rush through practices without achieving very much.

When you have mastered the basic quality movements and strokes, your feeders can help you become faster by throwing each shuttle a little quicker.

Top level players practise faster than the demands of the game but it's best to learn how to walk before you run.

WEDNESDAY

The lob

The last forecourt stroke to look at today is the *lob*. It can be regarded as either a defensive or an attacking stroke, depending upon its trajectory and the situation in which it is played.

Understanding the use of each stroke in the game will make it easier for you to visualise its effect as you practise, so begin by considering the value of the lob as a move in the game.

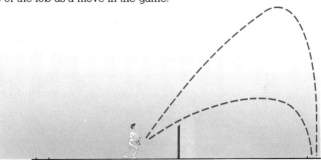

Trajectories for defensive and attacking lobs

The lob as a move in the game

As a defensive shot, the high lob can create time for you. The higher the shot, the more time you have to recover from whatever difficulties you may be in.

The high lob can have the same effect as the high serve, in that it can be used simply to move your opponent to the rearcourt.

The attacking lob can be likened to the flick serve, as it has a flatter trajectory and is used to get the shuttle low, preferably behind an opponent.

A practice for the attacking lob

Set up the practice in a similar way to the net shot practice, with your partner throwing the shuttle for you to hit. Return to the midcourt after each hit.

Keypoints

- Meet the shuttle early.
- Use the power from your wrist, forearm and fingers with little or no throwing action.
- Use the tap action.

The defensive lob

You need as much height as the hall allows without hitting the roof, so use your underarm throwing action for increased power, combined with a whip feeling as you uncock your hand, following the line of flight of the shuttle.

Since you will usually be using this stroke when you need to get out of trouble, your partner will need to put you under a little bit of pressure from the feed, making you hit the shuttle from close to the floor.

It's best to practise the movement first and then combine movement and stroke to give a realistic feel to the practice.

Begin from the middle of the half court and as you move forwards lunge onto your racket leg

Posture

You will probably have to reach towards the floor with your racket but you don't want to find yourself taking a nose dive, so bend your legs and retain your upright posture and balance. Since you have played a defensive stroke, take up a defensive stance facing the area that you have hit to.

Keypoints

- Hold your racket with a backhand grip, keeping it comfortably out in front of you.
- The backhand grip allows you to quickly hit shots from your backhand side and from in front of your body. You will need to change grip at speed for shots on your forehand side.

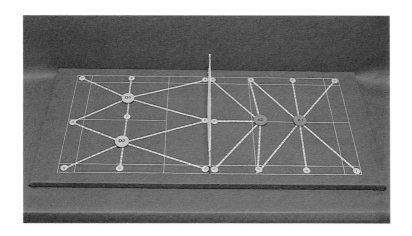

Areas of responsibility for players in attacking and defensive formations

Using the lob as a move in a game situation

To help you combine the defensive lob practice with your doubles positional play, your next practice will need four players.

The front attacking player hits the shuttle low over the net to make one of the defenders play a high lob, to force the back attacking player as far back as possible. By also taking the player out wide, the defenders create a space which they can hit into with their next shot.

The rearcourt player plays dropshots and smashes as the defenders lob.

The attacking side should always be on the lookout to punish any weak replies with the front player moving to intercept and kill or play a shot to keep the defenders under pressure.

Court positioning

So far the practices have shown the players in either an attacking or a defending formation. Within the game, the situation changes as both sides try to get into a winning position with each pair forming a team working with and for each other. Intelligent positional play is an essentia¹ part of the game.

The attacking formation

The side which has the opportunity to hit down takes up this formation with one player responsible for the front part of the court and the other player responsible for the back part of the court. The midcourt area is a shared responsibility and this may well be the area to exploit in competition.

The defensive formation

The court is divided lengthways down the centre with each player looking after one half. The players adopt this formation when the opposing side are in a position to hit down at them. They must decide who will take shots down the centre as this may well be a vulnerable area in a game.

Changing formations

To develop the change over from defence to attack, begin with players 1 and 2 on one side and 3 and 4 on the opposite side, all in defensive positions.

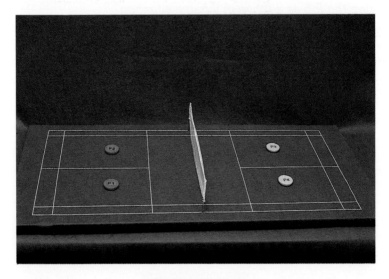

Starting positions

At the signal, *1 attack*, given by a helper, player 1 moves to a rearcourt position whilst player 2 moves to a point just behind the centre front service line, thus establishing the attacking formation. Players 3 and 4 remain in the defensive formation.

WEDNESDAY

The helper then signals for either 3 or 4 to move into the rearcourt attacking position with their partner simultaneously moving to cover the net with an aggressive stance. Players 1 and 2 must immediately revert to the defensive *sides* formation. The front player will normally drop back to the nearest half court leaving their partner to move into the vacant half court.

Your helper continues to call so that you can establish the habit of court positioning.

An alternative practice will direct one attacking player towards the net, leaving the partner to move into a position from which the mid and rearcourt can be covered.

The final court position practice will give the called player the choice of taking up either the rearcourt or the forecourt attacking position with the other players making the appropriate response.

Transferring the practice to the game

For these moves to happen automatically in the game, you will need to practise both set patterns of play and co-operation doubles in which the aim will be to develop your court positioning rather than your tactical knowledge.

Co-operation doubles

* Both sides begin in the attacking formation.
  The player serving serves high.
  The serving side move into the defensive formation.
  The receiving side move into the attacking formation.
  The attacking side play drop shots which the defending side lob until the attacking side clear and the roles reverse.
* Both sides begin in the attacking formation.
  The player serving serves low.
  The receiver pushes the shuttle back low over the net.
  A co-operation net rally develops with both sides in the attacking formation until one player lobs resulting in that side changing to defence.

Finish the day with some unrestricted doubles games.

You have been practising situations involving clears and lobs and generally slowing the game down to facilitate learning. Now you will want to play to improve and to win. In order to do so, you must follow the principle of attack within a fast framework.

Don't worry too much about mistakes. Obviously don't become careless or reckless but in a fast hitting situation, mistakes are initially inevitable. The only way to learn to cope with speed is to play at speed and with fast practices and fast games, you will eventually make fewer mistakes.

WEDNESDAY

An efficient doubles pair will know:

- How to create and maintain an attacking situation.
- How to defend.
- How to turn defence into attack (counter attack).

Attacking strokes
Smash
Disguised fast drop
Attacking clear
Net kill.
Net shot
Midcourt push

Defensive strokes
High lob
High clear

Counter attacking strokes
Drives
Low pushes or blocks

THURSDAY

DEVELOPING LEVEL DOUBLES PLAY

Today's Aims

Improve your defence;
Overcome your weaknesses;
Develop your midcourt strokes;
Find out how shadow badminton can help your game;
Learn more about level doubles.

Back to the wall

When you begin your hitting practices today, make use of the wall again but in a different way from before.

Standing with your back touching the wall forces you to restrict your backswing and encourages you to hit from in front of your body which is precisely what you must do at certain times in the game, particularly when you are engaged in a fast reaction rally which frequently happens in doubles

Whilst you have the wall behind you, your partner stands in a space opposite to you, about five or six strides away. Begin by pushing the shuttle between you, concentrating first on grip change, then on your racket face being square to the shuttle on impact and finally on varied racket head control by also using the tap action.

THURSDAY

The aim of the practice is to control the shuttle using the strength from your forearm, wrist and fingers. The shuttle will be coming at you fast and at different angles and you must learn to cope with all possibilities, so that no-one can catch you out in the game.

Begin each rally with an upward hit to your partner who hits down at your backhand, your forehand and your body, first in a known pattern but eventually in a random sequence. Try to return your partner's shots, not just by lifting the shuttle but by hitting it back flat as a means of turning defence into attack.

As soon as you get into the counter attack situation, keep your racket head up and use the overarm and sidearm hitting actions that you used earlier in your solo practice against the wall. As you get better, your partner can pressurise your defence by placing the shuttle accurately at your ankles, knees, shoulders and chest. Moving closer together to practise will really put your reaction time to the test.

Half court practice

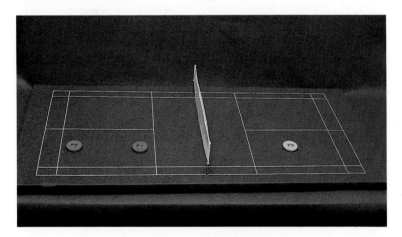

2 v. 1, attack v. defence practice

Next use the half court with two players in the back and front formation on one side of the net and one player in the defensive position on the opposite side of the net.

The single player hits the shuttle high to the rearcourt and takes up an alert, defensive position in the midcourt.

The rearcourt player attacks the defender who uses the skills just practised to return the shuttle quickly across the net.

THURSDAY

The front attacking player tries to intercept and hit down any shuttle that can be hit from in front of the shoulder line.

If the attacking side vary the pace and placement of their hitting, they should be able to force the defender to lift rather than give the opportunity to counter attack.

Each player will practise in each of the three positions.

Full court practice

Begin as you would in a game, with both sides in the attacking formation and try out the following ideas.

Low serve, low reply, net rally until one player lobs the shuttle high and that side defends. This should be fairly easy for you since you did this in one of your court positioning practices. Don't forget that this is, at least up to this stage, a co-operation practice.

Now, as your opponent hits the shuttle downwards, your aim is to use your defensive skills to return the shuttle low into the side tramlines, thus beginning the first move to regain the attack from your opponents.

Push the shuttle low into the forecourt to try to force a lift. Push to the midcourt which may cause some hesitation between your opponents. Hit the shuttle hard and flat to the rearcourt to try to get a weak reply.

All four of you should work in each of the four positions.

Turn a weakness into a strength

By working and playing with and against different players, you will discover your own, and their, strengths and weaknesses. If you want to turn a weakness into a strength:

- practise the stroke on its own;
- include movement in the practice;
- practise the stroke in a game-related situation;
- use the stroke as often as possible in practice games, sometimes by arrangement with the opposing side.

Repeating practices

It's important to repeat practices. With any new practice, first get the feel of the situation. The next time though, concentrate on a particular aspect that will help you become better. Once you've mastered the practice, repeat it to maintain your level of performance or increase the difficulty if you wish to raise your performance.

THURSDAY

Midcourt strokes

If your side is attacking and the opposing side return the shuttle flat down the sides of the court, you and your partner will need fast feet and a range of strokes to maintain control and command of the game.

The front player on your side must hunt the shuttle at all times, should be eager to play the net kill and must be prepared to take chances without being reckless. Winning badminton is about percentage play so go for it.

The back player must cover any shots that get past the front player. The aim must be to intercept the shuttle as early as possible, so isolate and practise the possible replies from this situation.

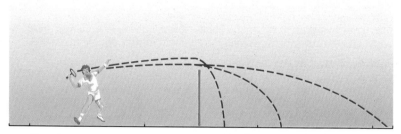

Develop a range of strokes from the midcourt to help you to keep the shuttle low, thus maintaining the attack

The strongest shot played from the midcourt is the drive. Use it to maintain the attack

THURSDAY

Setting up the practice

The shuttle must be fed to the midcourt tramlines at the appropriate height. This can be done by racket or by hand feeding. Whichever method you use, the skill of the feeder is crucial to your development.

Throw the shuttle like a dart

Safety

Safety is essential at all times. Sit on a chair or crouch so that your eyes are below net height, then throw the shuttle. Please note that the shuttle will be hit flat and fast across the net. You can protect your eyes by wearing goggles or by holding your racket in front of your face with your free hand.

Keypoints – Forehand drive

- Relax and imagine you are throwing a stone across the surface of water.
- Check your grip.
- Turn your body and step sideways with your racket foot towards the shuttle; you may need to use a preliminary chasse step.
- Bend your arm and cock your hand ready for a fast, wide sidearm throw.
- Contact the shuttle just in front of your body line, making sure that your racket head is above your hand and that your racket face is square to the shuttle on impact.
- Keep your eye on the shuttle.
- Use a tap or whip action to control your racket head.
- Use your leg strength to return to the starting point.

THURSDAY

Keypoints – Backhand drive

- Use the backhand grip.
- Turn your body towards the side of the court, stepping across with your racket foot, finishing with your back to the net.
- Keep your elbow low, your hand cocked and in one fast, continuous action, loop your racket head back and round, point the butt of your racket at the shuttle and throw your racket head towards it.
- Your forearm should have rotated and your hand uncocked.
- Remember to watch the shuttle as you hit it making sure that your racket face is square on impact.
- Push back to base.

Practising the drives

To practise the drive, begin by straddling the centre line in the midcourt.

Practise your forehand drive, concentrating on a keypoint of the action until you are satisfied that it's better. Perseverance will overcome problems but you may find it helpful to switch your attention to an alternative keypoint and return to the original practice later.

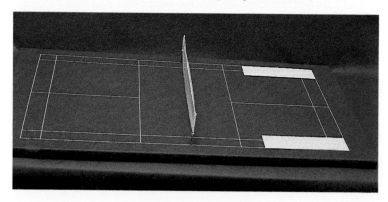

Target area for drives

For the time being, make the straight back box your target area. In the game, this will draw an opponent to the limits of the court and open up space in other parts of it. However, don't lose sight of the quality of your stroke in your eagerness to hit the target. Skimming the tape is the priority target.

THURSDAY

Practise your backhand drive and then combine forehand and backhand drives in the same practice. Use two feeders who will throw or hit alternately for you.

Developing this practice

You can make the practice more game-related by changing it to a decision making practice. Be ready on your base, legs bent, heels slightly off the floor, eyes and racket alert, ready to spring into action the moment either feeder releases the shuttle.

The fourth player in your group can control the feeders by standing safely behind you and pointing at random to the next feeder

Varying the stroke

Once your opponents realise that you are capable of leaving them stranded by the speed and accuracy of your drives, they may start anticipating them. This will leave the way open for you to play more subtle alternatives; the push to the midcourt or the push to the forecourt.

Make sure that you base these strokes on the same principles as the drives so that your opponents are kept guessing as long as possible because they are unable to detect which shot you are going to play.

Midcourt push

In this stroke the name of the stroke and the action used are the same.

Prepare as if to drive the shuttle but, as late as possible, control your racket head by keeping your hand cocked and guide the shuttle low over the net, to the area just beyond the front service line, where it may cause confusion between two attacking players.

Block to the net

Make exactly the same preparation but again check the action, this time with a short push tight over the net.

In order to get the shuttle to drop close to the net, use the racket face to direct the shuttle slightly upwards, remembering to keep your racket head above your hand.

Where to block to

Tactics must relate to your opposition. Although there are certain guidelines, these must be used in conjunction with your awareness of where your opponents are at the moment you hit the shuttle.

If your opponents are in a back and front formation, block straight to the side tramlines unless the front player is over committed to this shot in which case a cross court block may be a viable shot.

If the opposition is in a sides formation, consider playing your block to the centre of the net area. A moment's hesitation as to which player should go for this shot gives a tactical advantage to your side.

Practise each of the midcourt strokes on both your forehand and your backhand, so that you can control a fast shuttle to any part of the court.

Practising using the block in the game

Work as a four, beginning each rally from the defensive formation on both sides. Begin each rally with a long flat hit, a sort of extended low serve. Rally with fast, flat shots until you block to the centre of the net area to gain the attack for your side.

Remember that the aim is to make your opponent play the shuttle from as near to the floor as possible.

THURSDAY

Covering the probable replies

Since the probable replies to an effective block will be a net shot or
a lift, follow in towards the net with your racket up, to kill anything
played back to the net, leaving your partner to deal with the lifted
shuttle.

During your attack, if the opposition is able to get back into a flat hitting
rally, revert to sides and continue as before.

Improving movement in doubles

Shadow badminton is a useful practice for all levels of play. Learn how to
move fluently with forwards and backwards running steps, chasse
movements, jumps, twists and turns interspersed with stops and starts
and changes of direction.

Awareness of good posture and balance is essential at all times. In the
learning situation work at medium pace, the emphasis being on getting it
right.

For the more experienced player, polishing your body skills through
shadow badminton will prevent sloppy habits creeping into your game.
For all players shadow badminton can be a form of specific fitness
training, since the duration and the pace can be controlled.

How to practise shadow badminton for doubles

Since the emphasis today is on doubles, the shadow badminton will
relate to set areas of the court that you will have to cover within your
game.

First practice

Work from just behind the T moving to play imaginary net kills and net
shots anywhere along the net, returning to your base position between
each hitting action. Chasse and step or jump towards the sides of the
court as if you are trying to intercept shuttles travelling flat across the
net.

Work to a time limit and rest for three times as long. Twenty seconds
work followed by sixty seconds rest will give you time to compose
yourself, think about what you are doing and prepare for the next work
period. Active rest is best for your body, so walk around the court area
until it's time to restart.

THURSDAY

Keypoints

- Concentrate on moving smoothly and softly.
- Remember to finish with your racket leg towards the shuttle, except when you jump out sideways to your non racket side. With your racket, reach across in front of your body to intercept on your backhand or reach across behind your head to intercept on your forehand.
- Concentrate on keeping your back straight and your head up for good posture and balance both as you move and as you shadow the stroke from a poised position.
- Concentrate on how you carry your racket between shots. This will vary according to where the shuttle is coming from in the game but as the front attacking player, you must keep your racket in a high position in the forecourt.

Duration of practice

Four sets of work with the focus on one keypoint for each set before you move to practise the same qualities in a different court area will benefit your badminton.

You will feel physically and mentally stimulated, particularly if you adopt a dynamic approach but remember to stay relaxed. Tension in any part of your body, particularly in your grip, will inhibit the flow of your game.

Second practice

Travel from your base into the rearcourt and midcourt, moving into the areas that you will have to cover as the back attacking player.

The keypoints remain the same, except for the second point. At the back of the court, get into a balanced throwing position with your racket leg back. Put your whole body weight into the action.

Forehand or backhand

If in the doubles game the shuttle is lifted high towards your backhand corner, it's best to use your forehand overhead strokes rather than play high backhands, simply because you don't have to turn your back on your opponents and your peripheral vision will remain unimpeded. Being aware of your opponents at all times is crucial to your tactical decisions.

Don't assume that you can forget or neglect your high backhand strokes. You can bet that your opponents will be plugging away at this area of your game and you will need to be strong here if they are skilful enough to make you use it. However, you can learn about the high backhand

THURSDAY

strokes and related movements later and you will be able to incorporate these into your shadow badminton, although your forehand will remain your priority.

Third practice

Cover the whole of a half court as a defender. Combine movements to the front and to the back of the court, limiting your imaginary strokes to lobs and clears from which you assume a defensive role.

In the midcourt, one step on to the nearest foot will allow you to reach the shuttle in your half court.

In this defensive situation, play off the nearest foot and recover instantly for the next shot

Fourth practice – developing your partnership

Your court relationship with your partner needs to be both mentally and physically harmonious. Look first at the physical aspects.

As you move around the court and as the game changes from defence to attack and vice versa, you will find yourself moving around and inter- changing positions with your partner. You've already practised the simple attack/defence positions like this. Now take this a step further.

Begin in the attacking formation. As your partner moves to play an imaginary net kill or net shot, you, the rearcourt player, cover the diagonally opposite rearcourt shot. Both of you return to your respective bases.

This continues with your front player effectively being the leader, since you must respond to their movements. When you and your partner revert to a defensive formation, your partner can elect to return to the front, in which case the practice continues as before, or she can take over the rearcourt role, in which case you take over the front and become the leader.

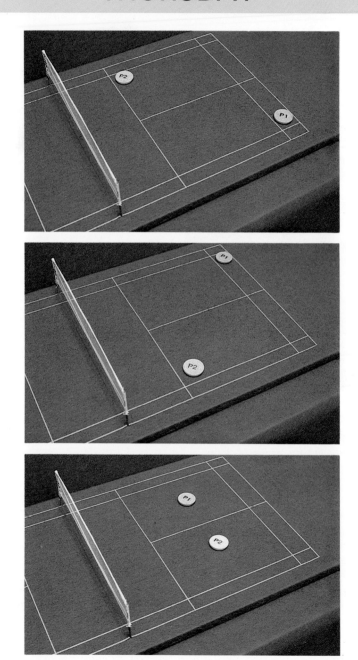

THURSDAY

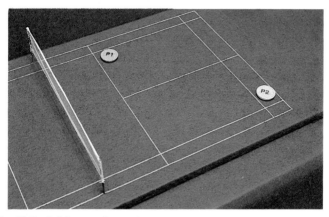

You'll find this practice quite demanding, even when you take it slowly, but you'll also find it fun

Communication is the name of the game

If you are to work effectively as a team of two, you and your partner need to know each other's game inside out. It will also be necessary to know who is the leader on the court. This may be one of you or it can be a shared responsibility but you must decide beforehand.

Hit player or set up player?

Decide where your strengths and your partner's strengths lie. In attack, how effective are you
– in the rearcourt?
– in the forecourt?

In these areas do you mainly try to set the shuttle up for your partner or do you go for the kill most of the time?

In defence, how effective are you
– in the right hand court?
– in the left hand court?

In these areas, do you mainly try to defend by lifting and hope that your opponents will run out of steam or do you make a conscious effort to counter attack?

Who has the best defence in your partnership?

Do you have to consider left and right handed players?

THURSDAY

Playing to strengths

Once you've considered these aspects, you can begin to play to your own strengths. If you are better in the front of the court, you must play shots that allow you to take up that position. If you are forced into a defensive situation and your partner has a better defence than you, lift the shuttle diagonally away from you to attract a reply to the strengths of your partnership.

To take advantage of playing with a left-handed player, consider serving wide from the right hand court to attract a reply onto your partner's forehand. In attack, try to place the shuttle to attract replies for your partner's left hand.

Consider also the strengths and weaknesses of your opponents and their preferred roles within their partnership. Try to exploit their tactical weaknesses as well as their technical weaknesses.

Attack or defence

Obviously, the game is a mixture of both attacking and defending shots but you are more likely to win if you play a predominantly attacking game, providing you can combine the qualities of aggression, patience and determination with speed, skill and tactical awareness.

Attitude

Mental toughness is often the deciding factor in an otherwise closely contested match. As well as taking care of your own game, you may have to help your partner through difficulties.

Every partnership has good and bad patches. An encouraging word may well help swing the game your way and may also make you a popular player who is never without a partner.

Order of serving

Complete the day by playing some doubles games. Check that you know the laws and how to work out whose turn it is to serve, etc.

If your side wins the toss and you elect to serve, the first server serves from the right hand court to the first receiver on the diagonally opposite side of the net.

If, having served, your side wins the rally, you win a point and the same person continues to serve but from the left hand court and to the second receiver.

THURSDAY

When you are the first server or the first receiver, you will always serve or receive from the right hand court when your score is an even number and from the left hand court when your score is an odd number. The reverse situation will apply to your partner.

At the beginning of any game, the side serving first is allowed only one server the first time round. When that side has lost a rally, the service passes to the opposite side, the player in the right hand court becoming the first server. When this first server has lost the right to serve, the second server serves to the next receiver.

It sounds a little complicated at first but you'll soon get used to the pattern as you play.

Service court errors – Law 14

14.1 A service court error has been made when a player:
  (i) has served out of turn;
 (ii) has served from the wrong service court; or
(iii) standing in the wrong service court, was prepared to receive the serve and it has been delivered.

14.2 When a service court error has been made, then:
  (i) if the error is discovered before the next service is delivered, it is a let unless only one side was at fault and lost the rally, in which case the error shall not be corrected.
 (ii) if the error is not discovered before the next serve is delivered, the error shall not be corrected.

14.3 If there is a let because of a service court error, the rally is replayed with the error corrected.

14.4 If a service court error is not to be corrected, play in that game shall proceed without changing the players' new service courts (nor, when relevant, the new order of serving).

FRIDAY

MIXED DOUBLES

Today's Aims

Learn the basic concept of mixed doubles;
Practise your flick serve;
Find out how and where to return serves.

Mixed doubles

The basic concept of mixed doubles assumes that the man is the physically stronger player with a more powerful smash than the woman. As a consequence, the man is better equipped to dominate the rearcourt most of the time. If this is true, then it seems logical that the woman should dominate the forecourt most of the time and should also be prepared to intercept any shuttles passing low through the forecourt to other areas.

Special practices are important to develop the techniques and tactics relative to each player's role

First practice for one man and one woman

Set up a continuous rally:

Man   Stand in the midcourt, straddling the centre line.
Hold your racket in front of your body.
Wait with a backhand grip.
Tap the shuttle low over the net towards your partner.

Woman   Stand just behind the T.
Step towards the net with your racket leg.
Tap the shuttle at your partner's body.

Second practice

To develop strength in your forearm and wrist, try the same practice with a head cover on your racket. You and your partner can take turns to use the cover so that the workload is not too much at once.

FRIDAY

Variations

Practices can be developed in a variety of ways according to the needs of the players and to meet the demands of the game. Develop the last practice:

Third practice

Remove the racket head cover and rally with your partner going flat out for speed and accuracy. Next vary the pace of hitting by occasionally using the push.

Woman Vary the angles and trajectories of your shots and mix shots into the side tramlines with shots into the body. Vary the length of your shots by hitting to both the midcourt and the rearcourt.
Man Move the woman out wide by playing to the side of the court. Mix shots tight to the net with low pushes to the midcourt.

Straight or cross court?

Follow the general rule of playing straight to create a cross court space in which to hit a winner and percentage-wise you'll win more than you'll lose. Unfortunately, inexperienced players, and some who should know better, are often too eager to go for a cross court shot before they have created an opening.

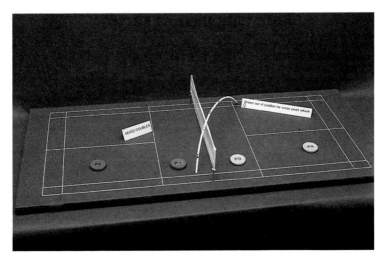

Pull your opponent out wide and create a space for a cross court shot

FRIDAY

Fourth practice for two men and two women

Play a conditioned game using low serves only. The aim is for each side to try to get an advantage over the opposing side using only net kills, net shots, drives and pushes.

Whichever side the man serves from, his partner should stand to the side of the T on his non-racket side

Returning the low serve

Thoughtful low serving, to get an advantage from the first stroke in the rally, is vital, but receiving serve is equally important. A shuttle recklessly hit into the net or out of court will give a cheap point to the other side; a weak, unnecessary lift will give the opposition an advantage.

Basic positions when receiving serve in mixed doubles

- Stand close to the front line, sideways on.
- Keep your heels off the floor, legs bent, in balance.
- Hold your racket up in front of you.
- Pick up the line of flight of the shuttle as soon as it is struck.
- Step through with your back foot and reach out with your racket to meet the shuttle as early and as high as possible.
- From your forehand court, receive shuttles served at your body on the backhand face of your racket. This will make it easier for you to hit to either side of your opponents' court.

Be adventurous, eager and competitive but don't be foolish. Try to make a winning shot from a poor serve. Play a safe attacking shot in reply to a good serve, so that you don't give an advantage to your opponents.

Rush or push?

You will need to practise returning the low serve with both a push action and a tap action. Use the push action for an accurate placement, tight to the net or low to the midcourt. Use the tap action to kill or to return the serve low to the rearcourt.

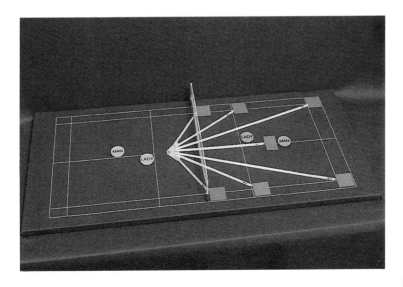

Target areas for return of low serve in mixed doubles

Practise the returns of the low serve

Get your partner to low serve to you and practise all the replies from both the right hand court and the left hand court. With continued practice on a regular basis, you will become confident that you can return any low serve to each of these areas. The woman's court position, when her partner is receiving serve, will be in front and to the opposite side of her partner when she is not very strong overhead in the rearcourt or if he frequently places the shuttle and seldom rushes it back fast.

If the woman is capable of controlling the shuttle effectively from the rearcourt, she will stand behind the man when he receives serve, thus allowing him to be more aggressive in his attack of service

Conditioned games

Now it's time to play some mixed doubles games. Each player will be limited to low serving, so that you can try out what you have practised.

Don't fall into the trap of allowing a seemingly aggressive receiver of serve to put you off your game. You must always have a positive

FRIDAY

approach. If you know that you have a good serve, once you've decided where to serve to, block the receiver from your mind and just imagine you're back on the practice court.

Flick serve

It's essential to have a disguised flick serve with which you can tame an ambitious player. Your flick serve will be obviously effective if it aces your opponent; it will also be effective if it catches your opponent off balance, particularly if it results in a weak or predictable reply.

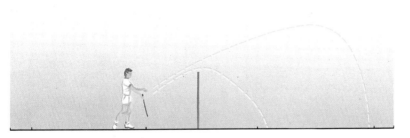

If your opponents are afraid of your flick serve, they won't be so keen to stand close to the front service line and this will make it easier for you to go back to using your low serve

Keypoints must be identical to those for your low serve, except that, as late as possible, uncock your hand to tap the shuttle over or past your opponent.

Practices

- Practise the stroke to get the feel of the action.
- Learn to flick serve with both forehand and backhand actions.
- Try out your flick serve against an attacker, who must not move before the shuttle is struck, since this is against the rules of the game.
- Now mix low and flick serves within the practice.
- Practise against male and female receivers.
- Note their replies and decide with your partner who will cover which replies.
- Complete each practice with the appropriate move on court to cover these replies.

Within your mixed four, play a modified game which will consist of a maximum four shot rally.

FRIDAY

The aims of the practice game are:

- to test the effectiveness of your serves;
- to find out if, after serving, your court positioning, in conjunction with your partner, is effective;
- to test whether your side can play an effective third shot;
- to decide which side has the advantage after the fourth and last shot.

Return of the flick serve

Be totally alert to recognise and counter any tactic that your opponent may try to use against you. To counter a good flick serve, you will need speed, strength and agility plus the necessary racket skills to place the shuttle to any part of the court.

Keypoints

- Prepare exactly as you did for the receive of low serve.
- Use the strength from both legs to push away from the floor to get behind the shuttle.
- Chasse, leap or use a combination of these to get quickly into your hitting position.

Practise the movement in isolation, concentrating stage by stage on the different components which, when combined together result in high level body skills.

Replies to the flick serve

Your level of play will determine the probable stroke moves that you make and, as you and your partner get better, you can review how you will play as a team. The following basic suggestions may help.

Man Smash or fast drop, followed by a move to a central base position to cover any replies which get past the woman.

The straight reply will usually be covered by the opposing man, whilst the cross court reply will normally be covered by the opposing woman.

An attacking cross court clear followed by a move to cover the straight replies or a returned cross court clear. Your attacking clear will possibly tempt the opposing woman to move back to take this shot. This may be a sensible shot to play for two reasons.

a) The woman will have a difficult shot to deal with.

b) She will be as far away as possible from her forecourt area of responsibility.

FRIDAY

Woman Smash or fast drop straight, followed by a move towards the net with your racket up.

Cross court clear followed by a forward move, leaving you in position, behind the front service line, to cover any downward cross court replies.

Rehearse the movement and shadow the strokes before you practise combining the movement with the actual stroke production. Take each stroke in turn and work on accuracy, consistency and quality.

When you are satisfied with your progress, you can repeat some of the earlier practices but you will have a different aim this time.

Repeat the practice with your partner, who can low or flick serve to you. This time however, your partner must flick a high percentage of the serves, since your aim is to test your ability to reply to flick serves.

Next, repeat the modified, maximum four-shot rally practice to test:

- The effectiveness of your returns of serve, in particular the flick serve.
- To develop, with your partner, your understanding of court positioning after replying to a flick serve.
- To test whether your side can get the advantage in the rally, having been flick served.

Mixed doubles defence

You have already included occasional clears in your replies to the flick serve and, if either you or your partner are forced into taking the shuttle from close to the floor, it may be necessary to lob the shuttle as high as possible to the back of the court, giving you time to assemble your defence before one of your opponents hits the shuttle. You will now be ready to counter attack.

Defensive positions

You will have realised that the defence positions in standard mixed doubles are different to those in level doubles, so set up some practices for you and your partner to get used to working as a team in this situation.

The woman has her racket up and is ready to pick off any attacking cross court shot and return it straight, into a space in front of her

73

FRIDAY

Practice for mixed defence

One player hits the shuttle high to a rearcourt corner to the opposing man. (NB This is not a serve but a preliminary stroke to get the practice under way.) Take up your defensive positions.

Man Position yourself to cover shuttles hit straight down the side, or hit down the centre of the court.

Your aim is to return the shuttle low, either tight over and close to the net or to the midcourt. Alternatively, drive the shuttle back fast and flat to the rearcourt. If you can beat the opposing woman with a cross court shot, then by all means do so. Otherwise, play straight to create an opening for a possible cross court shot next time.

Woman Position yourself just behind the front service line, diagonally opposite to the player hitting the shuttle. Use your high racket to block the shuttle to the forecourt, to push the shuttle low to the midcourt or tap the shuttle to the rearcourt.

Whichever shot you decide upon, play straight into the court space in front of you. Practise and become skilful with these replies and you will teach many a lesson to any man who plays an untimely cross court shot against you.

As with other practices, it's best to decide which reply you are trying to learn or improve. Rehearse this several times before moving on to the next one.

Follow these with a decision making practice before moving on to a competitive practice in which you play out the rally. For your final on court work, play some mixed double games. Plan your tactics to suit your strengths but be prepared to adapt your tactics according to different opponents that you encounter.

This woman is using crouch defence to counter attack against the opposing man

SATURDAY

DEVELOPING MIXED DOUBLES

Today's Aims

Learn to dominate the net;
Discover alternative mixed doubles;
Improve your net play – table tennis style;
Find out how to play brushed net shots;
Learn to use and reply to the drive serve.

Quality net play will give you an advantage in all three disciplines of badminton. To gain dominance of the net is to gain dominance of the rally, so look at a few ways of doing this.

Setting up the practice

Work in the half court on the opposite side of the net to your partner. Work first of all on speed hitting; flat, fast, tape skimming shots. Next, move forwards as you hit, so that you are gradually reducing the time between hits.

Whoever gets to the net first will be able to hit down at the other, thereby gaining dominance of the rally.

A high racket, a cocked hand, nimble footwork, a quick eye and a sense of adventure will help you to develop special skills that are valuable in doubles

SATURDAY

Developing the practice

Whenever your opponent is able to move in to dominate the net, your attitude must be positive. Don't chicken out and immediately lift the shuttle. Frequent use of your forearm and wrist will make them stronger and equip you to hit the shuttle back repeatedly flat and fast until you can change from defence to attack. Within this practice you will find yourself changing from underarm to sidearm to overarm hitting.

The aim of the practice is to change from a low racket to a high racket hitting position, from which you can move forwards to dominate the net.

It will be best to get the feel of the practice at first. To help you do this, follow these suggestions.

- Begin the rally with one of you at the net and the other towards the rearcourt.
- Set off with medium paced hitting.
- Treat the practice as one of co-operation.
- As the back player advances towards the net, the net player retreats towards the back of the court.

Once you are able to control the shuttle, step up the pace of hitting and moving and make the practice competitive.

Fitting the practice into the game

Imagine yourself playing mixed doubles. However, in defence, instead of leaving the man to take the bulk of the responsibility, because of your limited strength, you are now equipped to share that responsibility. You will no longer be limited to covering the cross court shots with the possibility of being exposed if you have to cover the straight shots. As a consequence, your partnership will have more variables and this will make it more difficult for your opponents to plan strategies against you.

However, your aim will be not simply to help out in defence but to take the first opportunity to get back into the front of the court, either to kill or to set up the shuttle for the man to hit down.

Begin the practice by hitting the shuttle high, deep and straight to the man who will hit the shuttle down. Your side must counter attack. The woman is now expected to move forwards to regain the attacking formation.

Remember that you must be equally competent on both sides of the court, so after you have practised in the right hand court change to practise in the left hand court.

For the final part of this practice, work in mixed pairs. Begin with one side defending and one side attacking, with the defending side using the advanced formation.

SATURDAY

The aim of the practice is for the defending side to regain net dominance, with the woman at the front.

Brush shots

If your opponents have a strong defence which is difficult to penetrate from the rearcourt, the winning shot in many rallies will normally be made from the forecourt.

You will need to learn to go for the kill on the net, not only when it is obvious and relatively easy but also when the shuttle has been returned tight on the net. Instead of hitting through the shuttle with your racket, as you would for an easy kill, you must learn to hit across the base of the shuttle, so that there is no danger of your racket hitting the net.

Place a shuttle upside down on the net. Old feather shuttles are best

Setting up the practice

Keypoints

- Stand behind the front service line, poised ready to move quickly, racket foot forwards towards the net.
- Use an action similar to a windscreen wiper action to brush the shuttle off the top of the net.
- Use your wrist and forearm, keeping the action small.
- Chasse back off the net, ready to repeat the practice again.
- Practise brush shots on both your forehand and your backhand.
- Watching the shuttle at the point of contact may well be a deciding factor in your success in playing these shots.

Net play – table tennis style

Although this practice does not reflect how you and your partner will operate as a doubles pair, it will give you the opportunity to sharpen up your net play, to use the standard net kill and the brushed net shot and make you think about where you are hitting the shuttle in relation to the position of your opponents. Above all, it's a great fun game which you will really enjoy.

How to practise

This is a practice for four players, two on each side of the net.

- Each player has five consecutive serves before the serve goes to one of the opposing side.
- Each rally must begin with a low serve.
- You are not allowed to play a kill on the return of serve.
- The shuttle must not be hit beyond the opposite front service line, except for the low serve and any net kill.
- Each player must hit the shuttle alternately with their own partner from their side of the net.
- At the end of each rally, the winning side is awarded a point.
- Play to 21 points or for a set time.

Consider:

- Where and how is the receiver standing?
- Does the receiver usually return with the backhand face or the forehand face of the racket?
- Will you serve forehand or backhand or will you vary your low serve in any other way?
- Where will you serve from?
- Where will you serve to?
- What sort of reply do you expect?
- Have you shared this information with your partner?
- Where will you stand when your partner is serving?
- Where will you stand when your partner is receiving?

Drive serve

Although it's undoubtedly essential to have a reliable low serve, your ability to deliver alternative serves will keep your opponents at bay.

You have already experienced the flick serve as a well disguised alternative, and next you will have the opportunity to practise the drive serve for the same reasons. The aim is to hit the shuttle fast and flat, with an element of surprise, into any gap that your opponent may have left open. It is probably most effective when played just above shoulder height down your opponent's backhand side. It is likely to have the greatest effect on a slow reacting player who is receiving serve in their forehand court. It can also be effective when played down the forehand, against an opponent who has moved too far across in their backhand court.

Keypoints

- Stand and look as if you are going to low serve.
- Keep the action identical to your low serve and indeed your flick serve until the last possible moment.
- Use a strong, sharp push action.

Practising the drive serve

It's not essential for you to have a partner to practise this or any other serve, although you will need a partner when you want to test the effectiveness of your serve.

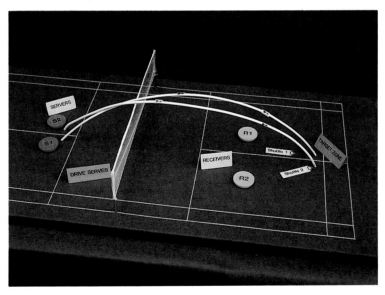

Try to hit the shuttle flat into the target zone. If you can get the shuttle behind your opponents, you may be able to limit their replies

SATURDAY

Place a lot of shuttles close to the side of your feet, so that you can practise many serves in a short space of time. Since you only have one shuttle in your hand when you play, make sure that you practise in the same way.

Returning the drive serve

In this cat and mouse game, you are constantly learning how to trap your opponent and, at the same time, learning how to get out of the trap, should they strike the first blow. A common strategy would be to drive serve down an opponent's backhand.

If your opponent uses the drive serve against you, you will need to be alert, fast and flexible, both with your body and your racket to reply. Develop a range of replies, so that your opponent cannot predict which you will use.

Player returning drive serve using round the head action

Round the head return of serve

Keypoints

- Check your forehand grip.
- Move back and reach across and behind your head with your racket; get the feeling of throwing it across to your non racket side.
- Take your weight predominantly on your non-racket leg.
- Control your racket head according to the shot you wish to play.

SATURDAY

Setting up the practice

Stand in the same position that you would stand in to receive a low serve. Don't be tempted to stand further back just because you know what's happening. The practice can only be of value if it helps you in the game.

Your partner now drive serves down your backhand. Your aim is to intercept the shuttle and place it accurately away from or at the body of your opponent.

Returning the drive serve on your forehand

Deliberately leaving a space can be a tactical move on your part, either in this or any other situation. By doing so, you are trying to invite your opponent to play into that space

Keypoints

- Bent legs; alert mind; racket ready.
- Aim to intercept the shuttle as early as possible and in front of your body line.

Practise returning the shuttle to all areas of the court with the full range of strokes.

SATURDAY

Conditioned game

Now that you've practised playing and returning the drive serves, play a game in which both sides can low or drive serve, so that you learn what the likely replies will be and which ones you will be responsible for.

Tournament

If you are learning within a group situation, a mixed doubles tournament will provide an exciting and enjoyable end to the day.

Goals

Before you play in any competition, it's a good idea to decide what your goals are, so that you can assess your results afterwards.

Here are some possible goals; study them and decide which order you feel is most suited to you.

- To improve.
- To win.
- To enjoy yourself.
- To play to the best of your ability.

Game etiquette

Most badminton matches are played without an umpire. Players are responsible for making fair decisions relating to the rules.

Give line decisions for your half of the court and accept those given by an opponent concerning their half.

If you hit the shuttle into the net or if it lands on your side of the court, return it to the next server.

Immediately call any fault such as hitting the net or double hit.

It is an accepted part of the game to hit the shuttle at an opponent. If the shuttle contacts the body of an opponent, it is courteous to apologise.

After a game, shake hands with the opposition and, if applicable, your partner, and thank anyone who has been involved in the organisation of the game.

SUNDAY

SELF DEVELOPMENT

Today's Aims

Assess your accuracy and consistency;
Develop round the head strokes;
Learn the technique for overhead backhand strokes;
Find out about sliced shots;
Improve your speed;
Learn how to change pace;
Assess your fitness;
Prepare for competition;
Find out how you can continue to progress.

Since today is the last day of your week of badminton, you can revise and improve your racket and body skills and add a few remaining skills to your repertoire.

After the warm up, begin with practices for accuracy and consistency, which are essential at all levels. Without these, you will find it difficult to assess whether your tactics are viable.

Badminton is a game of judgement and each time you hit the shuttle, you have to judge the height, length and the angle of the stroke.

For each stroke, prepare your body, prepare your racket and strike the shuttle with precision at the selected target. Be mentally strong and keep your mind constantly on your task.

Develop a routine

It's sensible to have a structured programme when you practise. In this way you won't neglect any area of your game. In order to measure your progress, keep a record of your practices with information on your accuracy, consistency and your own evaluation. (See page 84.)

Your programme will include:

- Hitting actions.
- Stroke practice.
- Routines.

2 v. 1 practices

An excellent way of setting up a challenging practice is to have two players combining to work for the benefit of a third player. In a group of three, rotate until each of you has practised from all three positions before moving on to the next practice. Each person in the group sets

SUNDAY

Personal assessment record

PRACTICE	DATE	DATE	DATE	DATE	DATE	DATE	DATE
1							
2							
3							
4							
5							
6							
7							
8							

RECORD YOUR BEST SCORE

SUNDAY

their own target for each practice, e.g. 10 repetitions without a mistake and then move on to 15, 20, etc. In your eagerness to improve your score, don't fall into the trap of sacrificing quality for quantity.

First practice – push action

Aim To experience the push action whilst keeping the shuttle low, trying to make your opposition hit the shuttle from as near to the ground as possible

Begin by pushing the shuttle to each other on a co-operation basis.

Gradually try to extend each other using the full width of the court and vary the length of the pushes between the net and the midcourt.

Be aware of the distance the shuttle has to travel to reach its destination and adjust your push action accordingly.

Check:
If the practice is not going as well as it should be, check out the basics – balance, eye on shuttle, grip.

Second practice – tap action

Aim To experience the tap action and to improve your reaction time whilst hitting flat and fast

Practise in the same formation as the first practice. Your judgement and the basics which affect this remain the same but you will have to make much quicker decisions.

Third practice – mix pushes and taps

Aim Combination of previous practices

Within the limitations of this practice, the two players should extend you in as many ways as they can without making the reply impossible. In this way you will have to push back any physical or mental barriers which will inhibit your performance.

Fourth practice – push, tap, whip

Aim To experience the different feelings in your muscles as you use each of these actions

Mix pushes and taps as before and occasionally use the whip action to send the single player towards the rearcourt. Keep the practice continuous, recording the number of successful hits made when you are the single player.

Fifth practice – forehand overhead clears, drop shots and underarm lobs

Aims To improve quality and quantity

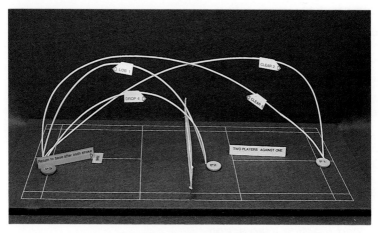

2 v. 1 in a half court practice

When you are the single player, practise alternate clears and drops against the opposing pair. The back player will return your clear with another clear, whilst the front player will return your drop shot with a lob.

After each shot, move to a central base and take up either the defensive or the attacking stance according to your shot.

Sixth practice – net play

Aim To improve control at the net

Use 2 v. 1 across the width of the court. The single player can use net shots and net kills whilst the other two are limited to net shots only.

For recording purposes, the single player's score remains continuous, even after a successful kill on the net.

Seventh practice – drives

Aim To practise the drives using
a) a one step approach and
b) a travel and lunge approach

Stay in the 2 v. 1 formation using the width but operate from the midcourt. Drive the shuttle flat and fast between you. When you are on the side with two players, your drives should be straight and down the side tramlines. You will probably need only a one step approach, so play the shot off the nearest leg to the shuttle. When you are on your own, you have the choice of playing a straight or a cross court drive.

For greater control and recovery, use the half lunge. When you are stretched further, use the standard lunge

Eighth practice – smash/block

Aims To control the shuttle with a mixture of power and touch

This is a fairly strenuous practice, so one person from your three can rest, whilst one works and one feeds.

Use the half court with the feeder in the midcourt playing alternately a lob to the rearcourt with a block to the forecourt. As the worker your aim is to get behind the shuttle, smash and move forwards to meet the shuttle as early as possible, pushing it back tight and close to the net.

In this routine, you will know that your feeder will reply to your net shot with a lob. Don't chicken out by immediately running to the rearcourt after you have played your forecourt shot. Be brave, chasse back off the net, maintaining your attacking stance. When the shuttle is hit, turn your body fast and use your leg strength to travel to the back of the court.

Quality

Stop the practice when you can no longer maintain your quality, accuracy and consistency. Over a period of time, you will be able to increase the duration.

After being the worker, you become the feeder. In this way, you'll learn to hold your skills together when you are tired and you won't be tempted to follow your natural instinct to flop down at the side of the court.

SUNDAY

By the time it's your turn to rest, you'll be amazed at how much you have recovered. Fairly strenuous work is normally done in the ratio of one period of work to three periods of rest. This will be approximately right in this practice, allowing for change-overs but you can always adjust the practice to suit your needs.

Further round the head practice

Whenever your opponent plays the shuttle high to your backhand side, you will have to decide whether to play a backhand shot or a round the head shot. Factors affecting your decision will be your position on court, your speed around the court and your strengths in these strokes. You have already practised round the head shots in reply to a drive serve, so you can now extend that practice. It is necessary to have an accurate feeder who can hit the shuttle with precision.

Begin with the smash, then play dropshots and then play clears. When you consider that you need to be able to play each of these shots to a range of areas, you'll realise that this is quite a lengthy practice. Keep your concentration all the time.

Alternate with your partner and discuss the likely replies from the various shots and your subsequent court positions. Continue with the habit of finishing any practice with the appropriate move on the court.

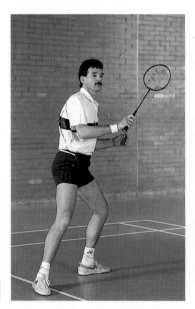 

Practise the movement first and then practise moving and hitting

Overhead backhand

The backhand can be taken in front of the body but your opponent will try to get the shuttle behind you

If the shuttle gets behind you, use a multi-purpose grip

SUNDAY

Backhand clear

Keypoints

- Check your grip.
- Relax your arm across your body.
- Loop your racket head round, aiming the butt of your racket at the shuttle.
- Rotate your forearm and uncock your hand as you 'throw' your racket high to 'tap' the shuttle on its way. (Try the whole action first of all without the shuttle, so that you get the feel of it.)
- If necessary try any part of the action that you may be unsure of.
- Try the whole action again and when it feels comfortable, get your partner to hit the shuttle high into your backhand and try it out.

For other backhand strokes, e.g. drop and smash, vary your point of contact and your hitting action.

Sliced shots, cut shots, spinners and tumblers

You may have noticed that some players occasionally hit the shuttle with the racket face at an angle to the shuttle, rather than square to the shuttle.

slice   reverse slice

There is no reason why you shouldn't try these out but it's best to have mastered the basic hitting technique of the racket face flat to the shuttle before you include these in your game

SUNDAY

The action of hitting the shuttle with an oblique racket face can

- cause the shuttle to rotate;
- create deception on length;
- create deception on direction.

For those of you who have played tennis or table tennis, you might have experience of these actions, although you will find that the shuttlecock behaves differently from the sphere.

Fast feet

Speed around the court may seem an obvious requirement to give you an advantage in the game; speed off the mark may not be quite so obvious but is the key to the former.

Go through a few exercises to help develop the fast twitch response in your muscles as well as generally stimulating your whole body and mind into fast mode. (See also next page.)

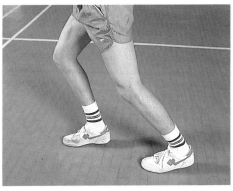

Change of pace

You can change the pace of hitting the shuttle and you can change the pace at which you move within a rally. You may be forced to change pace to reach a shuttle which your opponent has placed away from you. You can change pace to take advantage of a reply, so that you gain or maintain the attack. You can change pace to meet the shuttle early, giving your opponent less time between shots.

These changes of pace can upset your body system unless you have practised, thus preparing your body to be able to cope with the demands of the game.

Ways in which you can prepare for change of pace

Move around the court playing shadow badminton until you have played 12 imaginary shots.

As with your accuracy/consistency practices, go for quality rather than quantity. You can increase the number of shadow strokes gradually.

- Move at medium pace throughout the first set of 12.
- In the second set, move as fast as you can towards the imaginary striking position, returning to your base at medium pace.
- In the third set, move at medium pace towards the striking point and return at a fast pace to your base.
- In the fourth set, make your own decisions as to when you change pace.

SUNDAY

Fitness for badminton

Practising and playing will undoubtedly improve your level of fitness and this may be sufficient for your level of play. If, however, you find that your lack of fitness is detrimental to your game, you may wish to supplement your court work with some off court training.

Just as learning to play badminton as a member of a group brings rewards outside the game, so it is with fitness work. Join a class or work with a friend; seek advice, but as a general guideline include the 'S' factors in your programme.

- Stamina
- Strength
- Speed
- Suppleness

Although these 'S' factors are important, none are as important to your early badminton development as the main 'S' factor, *skill*.

Finish your day with lots of games, approaching them in the same professional way that you have approached your whole week of badminton.

Preparation for play

Mental preparation

It's always a good idea to prepare mentally beforehand, for the game you are going to play. Find a quiet corner and think about the tactics you are going to use and the strokes you will play. Visualise yourself moving smoothly, playing efficiently and above all remaining cool, calm and collected. If you are playing doubles, talk about the game with your partner.

Physical preparation

Warm up and stretch before you go onto court, so that you are ready to commit yourself wholeheartedly from the start of the game. The knock-up is the final opportunity for you to rehearse the strokes that you will need in the game.

The percentage use of the range of strokes in singles will be different to those in doubles, e.g. in singles, greater use will be made of the high serve and clears, whereas in doubles low serving and downward hitting will be more frequently used.

SUNDAY

Personal pride

Always play with good spirit. Acknowledge your opponents' good shots but be determined to throw every ounce of energy into returning them, so that you leave the court a winner, irrespective of the result.

Relaxation

As you are warming down, consciously relax your muscles and your mind, gradually slowing down your system.

Progressing further up the badminton ladder

Hopefully, after your week of badminton, you will have many happy memories as well as an understanding of how to play and practise. If you want to broaden your horizons even further and increase your knowledge, here are a few suggestions.

- Take the opportunity to watch better players.
- Your county association secretary will be able to supply you with a list of county events. Nationally organised events are staged at venues around the country.
- Join a club. Your county secretary will give you details of your area secretary.
- Enter a tournament. Most areas hold level and handicapped tournaments.
- Watch a video. Details are available from BAE.
- Continue to practise regularly and play games formally or informally.

Above all, *play for the love of the game*.

GLOSSARY

active rest   after strenuous activity, the recovery is aided by stretching and/or walking round

attack   hitting **down** into the opponents' court

base   the domed end of the shuttle; tactically, the position returned to after a stroke

bevel   the angled edge between the horizontal and vertical sides of the racket handle; a guideline in placing the hand

block   when an opponent smashes at you, a small movement of the racket head returns the shuttle low over the net

brush   a small, delicate sideways movement of the racket face as in moving a lock of hair from the forehead

chasse   'to chase'; movement in which one foot is moved sideways, then the other is moved alongside it

clear   a return high to the rearcourt – overhead or underarm
defensive clear – very high, allowing recovery time
attacking clear – lower, putting pressure on an opponent who has been brought forwards
standard clear – between those above

cock the hand   from a 'shake hands' position, use the flexibility of the wrist to move the fingers backwards and upwards

conditioned game   place an emphasis on aspects of the game by having certain adjustments to the rules, e.g. 'no smash'. Players must seek other ways of winning

counter attack   when an opponent hits down at you, take the shuttle early and high and return it flat or downwards

crouch defence   lower the height of the racket face by bending at the knees and intercept the attack; useful for counter attack

double hit   two contracts with the shuttle, usually created by the front player in doubles making a slight contact with the frame but the shuttle travels on backwards to be returned by the partner. Fault

dragging   during service, a player moves a foot along the floor. Fault

drive   a strong, flat stroke with the shuttle passing low over the net

drop   the shuttle is contacted high and hit downwards to land in the opponents' forecourt

fault   an error in play

feeder   a player who co-operates in a practice by hitting shuttles to a predetermined area

first server   in doubles, the player who starts in the right hand court and delivers or receives the first serve

flick   the action of uncocking the hand to create a sudden acceleration of the racket head, as in flick serve

hand feeder   a player who assists in a practice by throwing the shuttle

handicap tournament   player strength is assessed and officials attempt to arrange close matches with 'plus or minus' points

GLOSSARY

let   when a point has to be replayed, a 'let' is called
lob   an underarm stroke which lifts the shuttle high to the rearcourt
lunge   a long step

mental rehearsal   mental checking of skills of the game before the
   action
multi shuttle   a system of practising where the feeder supplies shuttles
   at speed

round the head   the shuttle is played on the backhand side with a
   forehand action

setting   a system for deciding the outcome of close games
shadow   going through a skill without hitting a shuttle

travel   indicating the player moves from one place to another on court